THE
MADONNA

THE
MADONNA

AN ANTHOLOGY OF
VERSE AND PROSE

LORENZ BOOKS

This edition is published by Lorenz Books,
an imprint of Anness Publishing Ltd, Blaby Road,
Wigston, Leicestershire LE18 4SE; info@anness.com

www.lorenzbooks.com; www.annesspublishing.com

Anness Publishing has a picture agency outlet for images for publishing, promotions or advertising.
Please visit our website www.practicalpictures.com for more information.

Publisher: Joanna Lorenz
Written and researched by: Steve Dobell
Project Editor: Joanne Rippin
Designer: Andrew Heath

© Anness Publishing Ltd 2013

Contents

~ ❧ ~

HANDMAID OF THE LORD
6

THE CHRISTMAS STORY
18

THE MADONNA & CHILD
32

O LADY OF THE PASSION
44

HEAVEN'S QUEEN
54

ACKNOWLEDGEMENTS
64

~ ❧ ~

~ CHAPTER ONE ~

Handmaid of the Lord

I often wandered
forth, more child than maiden,
Among the midnight hills of Galilee
Whose summits looked heaven-laden,
Listening to silence, as it seemed to be
God's voice, so soft yet strong, so fain to press
Upon my heart, as heaven did on the height,
And waken up its shadows by a light,
And show its vileness by a holiness.
Then, I knelt down most silent like the night,
Too self-renounced for fears,
Raising my small face to the boundless blue
Whose stars did mix and tremble in my tears:
God heard them falling after, with his dew.
Ah, King; ah, Christ; ah, Son:
Sleep, sleep, my kingly One.

ELIZABETH BARRETT BROWNING
"THE VIRGIN MARY TO THE CHILD JESUS"

*T*his is that
blessed Mary, pre-elect
God's Virgin. Gone is a great while, and she
Dwelt young in Nazareth of Galilee.
Unto God's will she brought devout respect,
Profound simplicity of intellect,
And supreme patience. From her mother's knee
Faithful and hopeful; wise in charity;
Strong in grave peace; in pity circumspect.

So held she through her girlhood; as it were
An angel-watered lily, that near God
Grows and is quiet. Till, one dawn at home
She woke in her white bed, and had no fear
At all, – yet wept till sunshine, and felt awed:
Because the fullness of the time was come.

D.G. ROSSETTI "MARY'S GIRLHOOD"

And in the sixth month the angel Gabriel was sent from God unto a city of Galilee, named Nazareth, to a virgin espoused to a man whose name was Joseph, of the house of David; and the virgin's name was Mary. And the angel came in unto her, and said, Hail, thou that art highly favoured, the Lord is with thee: blessed art thou among women. And when she saw him, she was troubled at his saying, and cast in her mind what manner of salutation this should be. And the angel said unto her, Fear not, Mary: for thou hast found favour with God. And, behold, thou shalt conceive in thy womb, and bring forth a son, and shalt call his name Jesus. He shall be great, and shall be called the Son of the Highest: and the Lord God shall give unto him the throne of his father David: and he shall reign over the house of Jacob for ever; and of his kingdom there shall be no end.

"THE ANNUNCIATION" LUKE 1, V: 26-33

Lowliest of Women, and most glorified:
In thy still beauty, sitting calm and lone:
A brightness round thee grew; and by thy side,
Kindling the air, a Form ethereal shone,
Solemn, yet breathing gladness. From her throne
A Queen had risen with more imperial eye;
A stately Prophetess of victory
From her proud lyre had struck a tempest's tone.
For such high tidings as to thee were brought,
Chosen of heaven, that hour: but thou, O thou,
E'en as a flower with gracious rains o'erfraught,
Thy Virgin-head beneath its crown didst bow,
And take to thy meek breast the All-holy Word,
And own thyself the Handmaid of the Lord.

FELICIA D. HEMANS "THE HANDMAID OF THE LORD"

My soul doth magnify the Lord,
And my spirit hath rejoiced in God my Saviour.
For he hath regarded the low estate of his handmaiden:
For, behold, from henceforth all generations shall call me blessed.
For he that is mighty hath done to me great things;
And holy is his name.
And his mercy is on them that fear him
From generation to generation.
He hath shewed strength with his arm;
He hath scattered the proud in the imagination of their hearts.
He hath put down the mighty from their seats,
And exalted them of low degree.
He hath filled the hungry with good things;
And the rich he hath sent empty away.
He hath holpen his servant Israel,
In remembrance of his mercy;
As he spake to our fathers,
To Abraham, and to his seed for ever.

"THE MAGNIFICAT" LUKE 1, V: 46-55

~ CHAPTER TWO ~

The Christmas Story

And all went to be taxed, every one into his own city. And Joseph also went up from Galilee, out of the city of Nazareth, into Judaea, unto the city of David, which is called Bethlehem (because he was of the house and lineage of David); to be taxed with Mary his espoused wife, being great with child. And so it was, that, while they were there, the days were accomplished that she should be delivered. And she brought forth her firstborn son, and wrapped him in swaddling clothes, and laid him in a manger; because there was no room for them in the inn.

LUKE 2, V: 3-7

In David's city, Shepherds, ye shall find
The long foretold Redeemer of mankind;
Wrapped up in swaddling clothes, the Babe divine
Lies in a manger; this shall be your sign.
He spake, and straightway the celestial choir
In hymns of joy, unknown before, conspire.
The praises of redeeming Love they sung,
And Heaven's whole orb with Hallelujahs rung.
God's highest glory was their anthem still;
Peace upon earth, and mutal good will.
To Bethlehem straight the
enlightened shepherds ran,
To see the wonder God
had wrought for man;

And found, with Joseph and the blessed Maid,
Her Son, the Saviour, in a manger laid.
Amazed, the wondrous story they proclaim,
The first apostles of his infant fame.
While Mary keeps, and ponders in her heart
The heavenly vision, which the swains impart,
They to their flocks, still praising God, return,
And their glad hearts within their bosoms burn.
Let us, like these good shepherds then, employ
Our grateful voices to proclaim the joy:
Like Mary, let us ponder in our mind
God's wondrous love in saving lost mankind.

JOHN BYROM "A HYMN FOR CHRISTMAS DAY"

Full of joy His beauteous Mother
Stood beside our new-born Brother,
        Who was cradled in the hay;
And her spirit's exultation
Thrilled her frame with sweet elation,
        To behold Him where He lay.

Oh! what deep, ecstatic feeling,
O'er the stainless Mother stealing,
        Marked the Sole-Begotten's birth:
How her soul's own silent laughter
Filled her gaze the moment after
        She first saw His face on earth.

Whose the eyes that would not measure,
Wonder-wide, that Mother's pleasure,
        Like to which no bliss hath been:
His in sooth were utmost rapture
Who one glimpse of her could capture,
        At her mother-play serene.

JACOPONE DA TODI

*B*ut see, the Virgin blest
Hath laid her Babe to rest.

Time is our tedious song should here have ending;
Heaven's youngest-teemed star
Hath fixed her polished car,

Her sleeping Lord with handmaid lamp attending;
And all about the courtly stable
Bright-harnessed angels sit in order serviceable.

JOHN MILTON
"ODE ON THE MORNING OF CHRIST'S NATIVITY"

When they had heard the King they went their way; and lo, the star which they had seen in the East went before them, till it came to rest over the place where the child was. When they saw the star, they rejoiced exceedingly with great joy; and going into the house they saw the child with Mary his mother, and they fell down and worshipped him. Then, opening their treasures, they offered him gifts, gold and frankincense and myrrh. And being warned in a dream not to return to Herod, they departed to their own country by another way.

MATTHEW 2, v: 9-12

*N*ow when they had departed, behold, an angel of the Lord appeared to Joseph in a dream and said, "Rise, take the child and his mother, and flee to Egypt, and remain there till I tell you; for Herod is about to search for the child to destroy him." And he rose and took the child and mother by night, and departed to Egypt, and remained there until the death of Herod. This was to fulfil what the Lord had spoken by the prophet, "Out of Egypt have I called my son."

MATTHEW 2, v: 13-15

~ CHAPTER THREE ~

The Madonna & Child

Mary sings: the ravished heavens
Hush the music of their spheres;
Soft her voice, her beauty fairer
Than the glancing stars appears:
While to Jesus, slumbering nigh,
Thus she sings her lullaby:

"Sleep, my Babe, my God, my Treasure,
Gently sleep: but ah, the sight
With its beauty so transports me,
I am dying of delight:
Thou canst not thy Mother see,
Yet thou breathest flames to me.

"If within your lids unfolded,
Slumbering eyes, you seem so fair;
When upon my gaze you open,
How shall I your beauty bear?
Ah, I tremble when you wake,
Lest my heart with love should break..."

ST ALPHONSUS MARIA DE LIGUORI

I sing of a maiden. That is makeless:
King of all kinges. To her Son she ches.

He came all so stille. There his mother was,
As dew in Aprille. That falleth on the grass.

He came all so stille. To his mother's bower,
As dew in Aprille. That falleth on the flower.

He came all so stille. There his mother lay,
As dew in Aprille. That falleth on the spray.

Mother and maiden. Was never none but she;
Well may such a lady Goddes mother be.

ANON "I SING OF A MAIDEN"

Herself a rose, who bore the Rose,
She bore the Rose and felt its thorn,
All Loveliness new-born
Took on her bosom its repose,
And slept and woke there night and morn.

Lily herself, she bore the one
Fair Lily; sweeter, whiter, far
Than she or others are:
The Sun of Righteousness her Son,
She was His morning star.

She gracious, He essential Grace,
He was the Fountain, she the rill:
Her goodness to fulfil
And gladness, with proportioned pace
He led her steps thro' good and ill.

Christ's mirror she of grace and love,
Of beauty and of life and death:
By hope and love and faith
Transfigured to His Likeness, "Dove
Spouse, Sister, Mother," Jesus saith.

CHRISTINA ROSSETTI
"HERSELF A ROSE, WHO BORE THE ROSE"

I say that we are wound
With mercy round and round
As if with air the same
Is Mary, more by name,
She, wild web, wondrous robe,
Mantles the guilty globe.
Since God has let dispense
Her prayers His providence.
Nay, more than almoner,
The sweet alms' self is her
And men are meant to share
Her life as life does air.
If I have understood,

She holds high motherhood
Towards all our ghostly good,
And plays in grace her part
About man's beating heart,
Laying like air's fine flood
The death-dance in his blood;
Yet no part but what will

Be Christ our Saviour still.
Of her flesh He took flesh:
He does take, fresh and fresh,
Though much the mystery how,
Not flesh but spirit now,
And wakes, O marvellous!
New Nazareths in us,
Where she shall yet conceive
Him, morning, noon, and eve;
New Bethlems, and He born
There, evening, noon, and morn
Bethlem or Nazareth,
Men here may draw like breath
More Christ, and baffle death;
Who, born so, comes to be
New self, and nobler me
In each one, and each one
More makes, when all is done,
Both God's and Mary's son.

G.M. HOPKINS "MARY MOTHER OF
DIVINE GRACE"

ℳother, is this the darkness of the end,
The Shadow of Death? and is that outer sea
Infinite imminent Eternity?
And does the death-pang by man's seed sustained
In Time's each instant cause thy face to bend
Its silent prayer upon the Son, while he
Blesses the dead with his hand silently
To his long day which hours no more offend?

Mother of grace, the pass is difficult,
Keen as these rocks, and the bewildered souls
Throng it like echoes, blindly shuddering through.
Thy name, O Lord, each spirit's voice extols,
Whose peace abides in the dark avenue
Amid the bitterness of things occult.

D.G. ROSSETTI "SONNET FOR 'OUR LADY OF THE ROCKS'
BY LEONARDO DA VINCI"

~ CHAPTER FOUR ~

O Lady
of the Passion

Now there stood by the cross of Jesus his mother, and his mother's sister, Mary the wife of Cleophas, and Mary Magdalene. When Jesus therefore saw his mother, and the disciple standing by, whom he loved, he saith unto his mother, Woman, behold thy son! Then saith he to the disciple, Behold thy mother! And from that hour that disciple took her unto his own home.

LUKE 19, V: 25-27

By the Cross,
on which suspended,
With his bleeding hands extended,
Hung that Son she so adored,
Stood the mournful Mother weeping,
She whose heart, its silence keeping,
Grief had cleft as with a sword.

JACOPONE DA TODI "STABAT MATER"

There stood also by the Cross of Jesus his most holy and ever-virgin Mother Mary... And how couldst thou stand? Whence came thy strength? Of a certainty, thy body was not of steel or stone, that this day thou couldst be pierced so many times by the sword of sorrow, and crucified so many times, and wounded together with thy Son, nevertheless thou didst stand there firm both in body and soul. Peradventure those strong and rough nails held thee also fast upon the Cross of thy Son, so that thou couldst not fall. Thou stoodest, therefore, the immovable column of the faith.

JOHN TAULER

O Lady of the Passion, dost thou weep?
What help can we, then, through our tears survey,
If such as thou a cause for wailing keep?
What help, what hope, for us, sweet Lady, say?

"Good man, it doth befit thine heart to lay
More courage next it, having seen me so.
All other hearts find other balm today –
The whole world's consolation is my woe."

ELIZABETH BARRETT BROWNING "O LADY OF THE PASSION"

O Lady Mary, thy bright crown
Is no mere crown of majesty;
For, with the reflex of his own
Resplendent thorns Christ circled thee.

The red rose of this Passion-tide
Doth take a deeper hue from thee,
In the five wounds of Jesus dyed,
And in thy bleeding thoughts, Mary!

The soldier struck a triple stroke
That smote thy Jesus on the tree;
He broke the Heart of hearts, and broke
The Saint's and Mother's hearts in thee.

Thy Son went up the angels' ways,
His passion ended; but, ah me!
Thou found'st the road of further days
A longer way of Calvary.

FRANCIS THOMPSON

~ CHAPTER FIVE ~

Heaven's Queen

Who is she that ascends so high,
　　Next the Heavenly King,
Round about whom Angels fly
　　And her praises sing?

Who is she that, adorned with light,
　　Makes the sun her robe,
At whose feet the queen of night
　　Lays her changing globe?

To that crown direct thine eye,
　　Which her head attires;
There thou mayst her name descry
　　Writ in starry fires.

This is she in whose pure womb
　　Heaven's Prince remained;
Therefore in no earthly tomb
　　Can she be contained.

Heaven she was, which held that fire
　　Whence the world took light,
And to Heaven doth now aspire,
　　Flames with flames to unite.

She that did so clearly shine
　　When our day begun,
See how bright her beams decline
　　Now she sits with the Sun.

SIR JOHN BEAUMONT

Daughter and Mother
and the Spouse of God
Alike of kin to that most Blessed Trine
Of persons, yet in Union, One, Divine,
How are thy gifts and graces blazed abro'd.

Most holy, and pure Virgin, Blessed Mayd,
Sweet Tree of Life, King David's Strength and
Tower,
The House of Gold, the Gate of Heaven's power,
The Morning-Star whose light our fall hath stay'd.

Great Queen of Queens, most mild, most
meek, most wise,
Most venerable, Cause of all our joy,
Whose cheerful look our sadness doth destroy,

And art the spotless Mirror to man's eyes.

The Seat of Sapience, the most lovely Mother,
And most to be admired of thy sexe,
Who mad'st us happy all, in thy reflexe,
By bringing forth God's Onely Son, no other.

Thou Throne of Glory, beauteous as the moone,
The rosie morning, or the rising sun,
Who like a giant hastes his course to run,
Till he hath reached his twofold point of noone.

How are thy gifts and graces blazed abro'd,
Through all the lines of this circumference,
T'imprint in all purged hearts this Virgin sence
Of being Daughter, Mother, Spouse of God?

BEN JONSON

Virgin most fair, who,
clad and crowned with sun
And stars, didst please the Sun supreme so well,
That for his light he made a tent in thee,
Love bids me something of thy praises tell,
But nought, without thy aid, can be begun,
And his, who loved thy body's guest to be.
I cry to one, who answers graciously
Whoe'er in faith implore.
If ever yet the sore
Sufferings of man have touched thy clemency,
Virgin, oh, now to my petition lean;
Do thou my warfare aid,
Though I be made
Of earth, and thou Heaven's Queen.

PETRARCH "ODE"

*H*ail Mary, full of grace,
the Lord is with thee:
blessed art thou among women,
and blessed is the fruit of thy womb,
Jesus. Holy Mary, Mother of God,
pray for us sinners now
and at the hour of our death.

Ave Maria

*W*ho could describe your splendour?
Who could tell of your mystery?
Who could know how to proclaim your grandeur?
You have embellished human nature,
You have surpassed the angelic legions,
You have surpassed all creatures...
We acclaim you: Hail, full of grace!

SOPHRONIUS OF JERUSALEM

After the most careful examination, neither as adversary nor friend, of the influence of Catholicity for good and evil, I am persuaded that the worship of the Madonna has been one of the noblest and most vital graces, and has never been otherwise than productive of true holiness of life and purity of character. There has probably not been an innocent cottage home throughout the length and breadth of Europe during the whole period of Christianity, in which the imagined presence of the Madonna has not given sanctity to the humblest duties, and comfort to the sorest trials of the lives of women; and every brightest and loftiest achievement of the arts and strength of manhood has been the fulfilment of the prophecy of the Israelite maiden, "He that is mighty hath magnified me and holy is His Name."

JOHN RUSKIN

Acknowledgements

The following pictures are reproduced with kind permission of the Visual Arts Library, London: p2: La Madonna della Salute by Padovanio, Venice. **p6:** Book of Hours: Annunciation by Bourdichon, New York. **p7:** Madonna and Child by Franciabigio, Birmingham Museum of Art, USA. **p9:** Holy Family with Saints in a Landscape by Rubens, National Gallery, London. **p10:** *(right)* Virgin in Adoration by Massys, Los Angeles. **p13:** The Virgin Praying by Sassoferrato, National Gallery, London. **p14&32:** Madonna and Child by Botticelli, Chicago. **p16:** Triptych of the Pentecost, Flemmish School. **p17:** The Immaculate Conception, Anon, New Orleans Museum of Art. **p19:** The Adoration of the Shepherds by Troy, Private Collection. **p20:** Merode Altarpiece, c1425, New York. **p21&37:** Madonna with Lilies by Botticelli. **p22:** Adoration of the Shepherds by Stomer, Nantes. **p23:** Madonna and Child, school of Memmi, Cleveland Museum of Art. **p24:** Holy Family by Bartolommeo, Los Angeles. **p25:** Nativity by Franken, Paris. **p26&55:** Maesta (Vierge en majeste) by Duccio, Sienna. **p27:** Nativity and Kings by Massys, New York. **p28:** Adoration of the Magi by Taddeo di Bartolo. **p29:** The Nativity by Schongauer. **p30:** Flight into Egypt by Bassano, New York. **p33:** Virgin and Child with St Anne by Leonardo, Paris. **p35:** Madonna and Child by Franciabigio. **p36:** The Gypsy Virgin by Titian, Vienna. **p38:** Virgin and Child and John the Baptist by Raphael, Paris. **p39:** Virgin and Child and John the Baptist, National Gallery, London. **p47:** Virgin of the Candelabra by Raphael, Baltimore. **p42:** The Mary Alterpiece by Van Der Weyden, New York. **p43:** The Virgin of the Rocks by Leonardo, Paris. **p46/7:** Crucifixion by Mantegna, Paris. **p48:** The Crucifixion by Van Der Goes, Venice. **p49:** Calvairy and donors by Massys, Antwerp. **p50:** Crucifixion Diptych, Virgin and St John by Van Der Weyden, Philadelphia Museum of Art. **p51:** The Deposition by Master of Frankfurt. **p52:** Pieta with Saints by Montagna, Vicenza. **P53:** Pieta by Van Der Weyden, San Diego. **p54:** Virgin, or St Rosalie of Palermo by Da Messina, Baltimore. **p56:** Polytych of St Zenon by Mantegna. **p57:** Madonna and Angels by Angelico, Frankfurt. **p58:** The Virgin of the Victory by Mantegna, Paris. **p59:** Virgin and Child by David, Philadelphia. **p67:** Virgin and Child with Angels by Massys, Courtauld Gallery, London. **p62:** *(left)* Pentecost, Unknown, French, Chicago Art Institute. **p62:** *(right)* Madonna and Child with Angels by De Coter, Chicago Art Institute. **The Bridgeman Art Library, London:** endpapers: Flight into Egypt, Fabriano, Galleria Degli Uffizi, Florence. **p3:** The Virgin in Prayer by Il Sassoferrato, Courtauld Institute of Galleries, University of London. **p8:** Immaculate Conception by Valdes-Leal, Museo de Bellas Artes, Seville. **p10:** *(left)* Annunciation by Gentileschi, Galleria Sabaudia, Turin. **p11:** Flight into Egypt by Caravaggio, Palazzo Doria Pamphili, Rome. **p12:** The Annunciation by Procaccini, York City Art Gallery. **p18:** Adoration of the Magi, German School, Giraudon. **p31:** The Flight into Egypt by Burne-Jones, Fitzwilliam Museum, University of Cambridge, Flight into Egypt by Fabriano, Galleria Degli Uffizi, Florence. **p44:** Crucifixion (alterpiece Church of S. Agostino, Siena) by Perugino. **p45:** Christ on the Cross from the Alterpiece of the Louvre, Paris, French School.